The Last to Leave

Selected Poems

DIRK VAN BASTELAERE

Translated by Willem Groenewegen,
John Irons and Francis R. Jones

Shearsman Books
Exeter

First published in the United Kingdom in 2005 by
Shearsman Books Ltd
58 Velwell Road
Exeter EX4 4LD

www.shearsman.com

ISBN 0-907562-70-1

Acknowledgements
The original texts of these poems appeared in the following publications:
   The Barnett Newman poems (see pages 65-69) were first published by
Druksel, Ghent, in 2003 in *De wind uit het elders. In praise of Barnett Newman.*
The film poems 'Soon at a cinema near you' (pages 73-83) were published by 234-
117 publishers, Ghent, in 2004 in the reading series *Het Rozenbalkon.* 'Wwhoosh'
first appeared in the journal *DW&B*, vol. 139 nº 5. Poems from *Pornschlegel en
andere gedichten, Diep in Amerika* and *Hartswederwaren* are published here with
the permission of Uitgeverij Atlas, Amsterdam & Antwerp.
   Some of the translations by Francis R. Jones have previously been
published online by Poetry International and Lyrikline at www.poetry.nl and
www.lyrikline.de respectively. Geert Buelens' introductory essay first appeared
in the yearbook *The Low Countries. Arts and Society in Flanders and the Netherlands*,
no. 12. (Rekkem: Stichting Ons Erfdeel, 2004 — www.onserfdeel.be). Our
thanks to the author and the editor for their permission to reprint the essay.

Flemish
Literature
Fund

The author and publisher gratefully acknowledge the
financial assistance of the Vlaams Fonds voor de Letteren
(Flemish Literature Fund — www.vfl.be) with the
commissioning of these translations. The publisher also
gratefully acknowledges the financial assistance of Arts Council
England with its 2005-2007 publishing progamme.

DIRK VAN BASTELAERE (1960) is one of the leading poets in Flanders. He came to prominence with his award-winning first collection *Vijf jaar* (1984) and then published *Pornschlegel en andere gedichten* (1988), one of the most hotly debated collections of Flemish poetry in recent times. This volume was to win for him recognition as the most important postmodern poet in Flanders. His work has been strongly influenced by American poets such as Gertrude Stein and John Ashbery and makes many references to contemporary art and culture, a fact which has led some critics to attack his work for its perceived intellectualism. The younger generation of Flemish poets, however, looks to him as mould-breaker. In 2000, he published *Hartswedervaren*, widely regarded as his finest book to date, and for which he was awarded the Flemish Culture Prize. His latest collection, *Zapruder Stress*, will appear in Amsterdam during the course of 2005. He has also published a volume of essays, *Wwwhhooossh. On Poetry and its Worldly Embodiment*; he is currently working on a second volume that will inlcude essays on photography, cultural politics/policy, Batman, *Cosmopolitan*, prostheses, choreographer Meg Stuart and J.G. Ballard's *Crash*.

WILLEM GROENEWEGEN (born 1971) is a bilingual (Dutch-English) poet and translator. He made his debut as a poetry translator in 2002 with a collection of poems by Arjen Duinker, published by Arc, entitled *The Sublime Song of a Maybe*. He has also published translations in various magazines, such as *Fulcrum Annual*, *Poetry Wales*, *Leviathan Quarterly*, *The Amsterdam Review* and *Poetry Review*. He is currently guest-editing a Dutch poetry special issue of South-African magazine *Carapace*.

JOHN IRONS lives in Odense, Denmark where he is a freelance translator from Danish, Norwegian, Swedish, Dutch, German and French. Before turning full-time to translation he lectured at Odense University and Odense College of Education. He holds a BA and MA in modern and Medieval Languages from Cambridge University and a PhD in Dutch, also from Cambridge, and a further MA from Lund University.

FRANCIS R. JONES is Senior Lecturer in the School of Modern Languages at the University of Newcastle-upon-Tyne. He translates from Dutch, Russian and Serbo-Croat, and has published volumes by Hans Faverey, Vyacheslav Kupriyanov, Ivan Lalic and Vasko Popa, among others.

GEERT BUELENS (born in Belgium, 1971) is a poet, critic and Professor of Modern Dutch Literature at the University of Utrecht. His second volume of poetry will be published in the summer of 2005. He is also working on a book about the Great War and European Poetry.

Selected Publications by Dirk van Bastelaere:

Vijf jaar (Antwerp: Soethoudt & Co nv, 1984)

Pornschlegel en andere gedichten (Amsterdam: De Arbeiderspers, 1988;
(2nd edition, Amsterdam / Antwerp: Atlas, 2002)

Diep in Amerika. Gedichten 1989-1991 (Amsterdam / Antwerp: Atlas, 1994.)

Hartswedervaren. Gedichten (Amsterdam / Antwerp: Atlas, 2000)

Wwwhhoooosshhh (The Opera Ain't Over Til The Fat Lady Sings)
(in: Peter Ghyssaert (ed): *Turkooizen scheepje van verschil: twaalf
jonge Vlaamse dichters*, Amsterdam: Prometheus, 1997)

Wwwhhoooosshhh. Over poëzie en haar wereldse inbedding (Nijmegen: Vantilt, 2001)

De wind uit het elders. In praise of Barnett Newman. (Ghent: Druksel, 2003)

Zapruder Stress (Amsterdam / Antwerp: Atlas, 2005)

CONTENTS

A Total Eclipse of the Heart

Geert Buelens

It is one of the pillars of Dirk van Bastelaere's poetry — and a crucially ironic one, I believe — that a poem is never self-evident. The same could probably be said of everyone, except for the odd dishevelled poetaster here and there, but I'm not talking about technical difficulties in rhyme-schemes or the search for the most appropriate metaphor. The problem this poet is struggling with is poetry itself. In a recent interview he said in so many words that "'haine de la poésie' — a hatred of poetry — (...) is vital for writing poetry". And this is no quip. Van Bastelaere is forever in search of the limits in everything. ('What then is poetry? Limit thinking'). Only when that ultimate frontier has almost been reached — might we be talking about death here? — can a poem become possible, can be a poem (again). He is trying to keep contemporary poetry alive by thinking it through thoroughly to the end.

One of the (perhaps unintentional) consequences of this radical stance is that van Bastelaere's poetry is heroic. The end is always looming, the apocalypse constantly about to boil over. But not quite. Is it mere coincidence that one of his essays is called 'That Batman Feeling' ('Het Batmangevoel')? Or that one of Virginia Woolf's sayings — 'Lines and colours almost persuade me that I too can be heroic' — is to be found in his most recent publication, a limited-edition chapbook dedicated to the work of Barnett Newman called *The Wind from Elsewhere* (*De wind uit het elders*, 2003). This twenty-six-year-old Batman (hero) once wanted to change the world. ('Because when Batman goes into action, the nature of reality changes'.) The poet as he speaks today is still striving for this in his own way, but his discourse has changed a couple of times since. Even though in 1989 he still spoke of his fascination with 'the secret that covers everything', 'judgment postponed' and his longing for 'change' and 'transformation', his key political text from that same year, 'Reef Building: A Small ABC' ('Rifbouw (een kleine abc)') speaks of deference, non-closure of interpretation and of flux as the only constant in existence. And again, ten years later, in an essay called 'Stay back, please' and also in the interview mentioned above, he talks about the 'real', of an ethics of desire (longing) and of a constant remobilisation of words and concepts. In the meantime, this intuitive comic-strip fan had read Roland Barthes and Paul de Man, as well as Maurice Blanchot, Jacques Lacan, Slavoj Žižek, Gilles Deleuze and Félix Guattari. His thinking had become more profound, re-evaluated and enriched by theory. But it is still guided by the star of a highly problematic, almost irresistible Absolute, an Absolute to be avoided absolutely but with which poetry may, can and must engage.

The missing whole

The climate in which van Bastelaere made his debut in the early 1980s was radically different from today's. Flemish poetry was going through a crisis: almost everything that the post-war period had brought forth in terms of experiment seemed to be succumbing to sterility, new names had far too hesitantly sought their place by the open hearth of complacency, risks were shunned and ambitions avoided. It was a new generation of artists that embraced the post-modern, like van Bastelaere (in poetry), Anne-Teresa de Keersmaeker and her company Rosas (in dance), Luc Tuymans (in painting) and Jan Lauwers and NeedCompany (in theatre), who dared once again to express their ambitions more sharply and also to realise them to a certain extent, without irony. Maybe that crisis was not as absolute as was thought at the time, but it remains a fact that the arrival of this new generation of artists was quickly felt by many to be the beginning of a new era.

Van Bastelaere's immediately prize-winning debut *Five Years* (*Vijf Jaar*, 1984) brought punk and new wave with it into Flemish poetry (viz. the quotes taken from and the poems dedicated to Joy Division and its lead singer Ian Curtis), along with the Berlin of David Bowie and the Red Army Faction. By using strategic quotations from Georg Trakl, Gottfried Benn, Hugues C. Pernath and Sylvia Plath, the poet positioned himself in a tradition that was anything but mainstream and suggested that the intertextual was unavoidable in contemporary literature. His collection can be read as a report of an adolescent crisis (who am I?) but also as a philosophical quest (what is 'I'?). He waded through the atmosphere of the Cold War, talked of No Future and of course of death, but also of the power of imagination and literature. His poems are dense, full of compelling and threatening images, a-syntactic constructions, or uncertain or vanished referents ('The fretful moon is her most beautiful / inflorescence'). Enter the poet, ambitious and totalitarian — like the communist five-year plan the title refers to. These traits would never abandon him.

Over-conscious as he is, van Bastelaere would thematise these traits. He would explain, illustrate and provoke, both in his poems — as in the often almost didactic *Pornschlegel and other poems* (*Pornschlegel en andere gedichten*, 1988), for which he was awarded the Pernath prize — and in his essays. The iconoclastic van Bastelaere self-confidently appropriated the critical apparatus of the day and used it to disqualify practically everyone who had anything to do with criticism and poetry in the Dutch-speaking regions. In particular, the Flemish professor and critic Hugo Brems and his friend Herman de Coninck, the most popular poet in the country, were to bear the brunt of this criticism. Not that van Bastelaere was insulting. He simply put them offside by shifting the goalposts of the debate on poetry. Consolation, empathy and the reconcilability of the world were rejected as regressive, even reactionary fictions. Readability became equated with saleability and mainstream poetry was considered a spineless component of capitalism. Other criteria determined Van Bastelaere's poetics: the gap between language and the world, a perpetually looming abyss, an alluring black hole, to be approached yet kept at a minimal distance.

The long title poem of his second collection does all this in a striking way. The opening line of 'Pornschlegel' has since become a classic: 'It's July, and who would kill for a woman now'. Oedipus, *Blue Velvet*, the brainwaves and nightmares of a museum attendant, many centuries of art history, and driving round Antwerp on a Vespa, etc., all crisscross each other. The poet himself adds instructions on suitable dosage: 'All parts of a whole that is missing'.

When his next collection, *Deep in America* (*Diep in Amerika*, 1994), contains no more allusions to commonly known paintings and its explanations are limited to sayings like 'It's life Jim, but not as we know it', important players like Benno Barnard and van Bastelaere's own publisher drop out. This collection is so hermetic

9

that they say it should have been called *Open Sesame*. The collection was published somewhat later by another publisher. It contains poems that perhaps invite a Baudrillardian analysis but that work without such theoretical apparatus. Their power of imagination is unequalled in Dutch-language poetry. Images, lines and almost endless meandering syntactic constructions unfold, bend and double only, it would seem, to fold back upon themselves. The result is deeply troubling and certainly not masturbatory. Deep in America, as the title poem puts it, 'is living the end'.

Such scorching insight also typifies the very long poem 'Wwwhhoooosh' (which previously appeared only in a magazine, and later on in an anthology), but this time all embedded in long quotations taken from German fascist tracts. What we experience here is the clash of two opposing absolutist systems: one driven by a total desire for power, a lust for dominion and conformity, and the other fired by the drive of a ubiquitous pop culture and an equally constant cultivated sense of contingency and ambivalence. As in 'Stay back, please', the essay mentioned above, the poet explores a highly dangerous obsession with totality:

> ... it is
> an example, it shows the power
> of sacrifice, displays resemblance and catastrophe
> and if you do not satisfy
> the desire demanded, you will die
> of a ravenous passion and rave
> while dying.
>
> *(translated by Willem Groenewegen)*

It is no coincidence that van Bastelaere refers here to the Flemish medieval mystic Hadewijch. 'Oerwoet' (a restless, almost ecstatic urge; primal frenzy) is central to her work. In her seventh Vision, she states that her intense longing to become one with God is so great that she 'stervende soude verwoeden ende al verwoedende sterven' ('dying would rage and in raging would die'). When you come so close to the verge of the Absolute (Life, Love, Poem), death is close by.

In his next collection *Happenings of the Heart* (*Hartswedervaren*, 2000), which was awarded the Flemish Culture Prize for Poetry, van Bastelaere literally addresses one of the central metaphors of our culture: the heart. Here it is not only the seat of emotion but also a romantic, literary, religious, political and philosophical motif. Again he writes of how life is generated by absolute desires but that ultimately death is always there. This is the case in the cycle of poems '18 oktober 1977' based on a series of paintings of the same name by Gerhard Richter about the Red Army Faction, but also in a series about Jesus called 'Fables of the Sacred Heart' ('Fabels van de Heilige Hart'). ('This was a mountain erupting out of its mountainness'). 'The heart of a heart is a heart attack' or so it says in the final poem: if there is mention of a core, then it is a negative one.

This negativity was responsible for the picture on the cover and also for one of the most important passages in van Bastelaere's collection of essays, which is also called *Wwwhhoooosshhh* (2001). In his essay on the Flemish poet Hugues C. Pernath, he writes: 'the core of Pernath's poetry is a fissured, ex-centric, eclipsed core, which is perhaps best rendered by an eclipsed sun. Not the imploded, insipid, risk-free, fake video sun of aesthetic postmodernism, but a sun that is emblematic of a poetry that is forever absent from itself, that comprises its own death and precisely from this draws its (ethical) power and vitality.' The sun is still there, but we can no longer see it as a simple sign of life and power. If we stare into the eye of the sun we ourselves are blinded. When the moon moves across it, only the shadow of the absolute remains and this too sucks and pulls us. This awareness of the absence of the sun is essentially ethical in nature. Negativity here is far removed from cynical nihilism; it stands for – and this applies to van Bastelaere as well – a conscious struggle with the problem posed by Adorno: how can we write poetry after Auschwitz?

The beginning is a continuation of the end

Among other things, the radical stance Dirk van Bastelaere takes in his work makes him the point of reference par excellence in Flemish poetry. Poets of an earlier generation (Stefan Hertmans, Leonard Nolens) see it that way, as do younger poets (Jan Lauwereyns, Paul Bogaert, Bart Meuleman, Miguel Declerq and others). Even though you may not agree with van Bastelaere, you still somehow have to adopt a position with respect to him. One of the striking side-effects of his fundamental theoretical structure is that practically all the studies of his work published so far use the premises put forward by the poet himself. And this too is crucially ironic: the poet who held forth on the rupture with heterodoxy has surprisingly subservient critics. Although he still regards himself as belonging on the margins (as can be seen, among other things, from the magazine he co-edits: *Freespace Nieuwzuid: Driemaandelijkse discursieve machine voor cultuurkritiek en amusement* (*Freespace New South: Quarterly Discursive Machine for Cultural Criticism and Entertainment*), in the meantime he has become one of the most prized poets of his generation and has, after some delay, been recognised in the Netherlands as being an important voice. He is, moreover, also strikingly popular among students of literature, both in the Netherlands and in Belgium. All this could be passed off as a remarkable form of repressive tolerance in bourgeois culture, but at the same time it points to a certain paradigm shift in literary culture. Van Bastelaere's poems have not yet found their way onto beer mats and bread bags, but 'Three Men and the Sea' (Drie mannen en de zee) will soon be written up on a promenade on the Belgian coast: 'I can be seen from the window / that will only let itself be known / once the man has crashed through it, / for such is thirst for knowledge.' (Translation by Francis R. Jones).

And so we arrive back at the beginning, which is a continuation of the end. Poetry will be radical or it will not be at all. It will deal with experiences of the edge or else make itself redundant. Poetry is not about recognition or empathy. It's about the afterwards, the always further, the beyond. '[H]ow does the poet relate to the mortality and futility in his poems? Isn't there something heroic to it?'

Translated by Peter Flynn

from
Pornschlegel en andere gedichten

(Pornschlegel and other poems)

Translated by
Francis R. Jones

Pornschlegel

I had intended to conquer the city and now
a palm leaf grazes past my head
Gottfried Benn

It's July, and who would kill for a woman
Now? It's so hot it's unreal. In the country:
A farmyard with some old plane-trees, thirty
In all. That's the age of the man who lives there,
A lovely guy, though he limps a bit in one
Leg, his left. Or so it would seem. Sometimes
He walks on one shoe. Whenever he thinks
About it he lies flat out on the floor, smashes
The watery mirror in the rain tank
Or turns his parents' photo on the sideboard
The other way round and stares silently into
Space. But now, as he looks up from the camp-bed
Where he's lolling – the morning already a-quake
With heat – on his forehead a couple of plasters still,
Now, at this very moment, as he looks
Towards the farmhouse, he sees the cherry orchard,
A cloud of noise, a swarm of starlings dropping
Into the trees, like grit. Is it a plague
Or a message? Is it significant, a new
Configuration? It hints at the branching of
Another reality into one's everyday life.
The starlings are starting to eat the cherries – they'll have
The trees stripped bare in no time. But Pornschlegel
The man has noticed nothing. He hears a motor
Mower drone, only the garden sprinkler
Hiss. Lethargic in the heat, sometimes
He spells his name. Soon he'll embark on his voyage.
Who would kill for a woman now? It's so hot.

He wanders into the room and yet another
Century. He's still able to fritter
Himself away in the familiar. 15th,

16th, he yawns (it's the day before the great
Heat, which will lie like a compress on the world),
17th century. He looks out of
The high window, sees the synagogue glitter.
The colour sweated by things seems mental to him:
Red of balcony flowers, blue of a patent
Leather shoe. The museum, floating on the
Afternoon, *is an Ionic island,*
Beautiful as a wreck from Paradise.
Inside, in half-light, the paintings and panels hang
As concrete as the images of a poem.
With all of this, Pornschlegel sometimes
Feels more unreal than what is portrayed. Sees
His foot dragging through the varnish of the
Parquet floor. He stretches his diaphanous
Hands before him: they are – still – his own.
Any moment now, other hands might
Appear in them. What's wrong with his physicality?
The fact that he's guarding shadows of paint (Cranach,
Memling, Patinir) is his daily bread.
He's just an attendant. But one portrait, which he
Worships, comes floating up in his dreams. It's Agnes
Sorel. And he knows who she looks like too. Portrayed by
Jean Fouquet as virgo lactans, she's an ivory
Skittle, hairless face and slim loins.
She's nature become idea and *'dame de toute beauté*
Parée'. She makes him part of history.
And in the already more evening light that's falling
And falling through the dome, she's calling him
To herself. The glass cracks and the century's empty.
He shuffles across the floor as if through water.
Her voice, very high, almost a flute note and surely
Guarded by seraphim and cherubim, comes
Like a finger out of the paint. She beckons. He nods.
She lisps and he sees her tongue, knitting-needle
Thin – 'See me or I perish' – and he
Hears: 'Free me and inherit'. That he
Has to break the glass to see the glass.
He thrusts his pearl-white forehead into the case.

He's found stretched out and broken on the floor.
And outside it's even hotter, empty and dry.

Sleep shows him a man on the Left Bank.
It seems like a dream in a dream in a dream. It's a plain
With the sun above. It's there and sometimes not.
The man walks across fields, across gravel. Along
A wall with broken glass on top. Panting.
He is searching or intending something.
Then the path runs out and the ground gets boggy.
He finds his way in circles to himself,
His purpose becoming wound around him. He walks
Past roots, between the stumps of trees – as if someone
Had to cut them down to save his life.
Here a phantom is someone *there* a walker
Wearing calfskin boots, though now there's a feeling
He might be fleeing. By an orchard stands
A scarecrow, straw-white hair sees blackbirds off
To another world. Cars come driving across
The landscape. The man has disappeared in a trice,
Partially shielded by foliage. The site is cordoned
Off with palings and red-and-white tape. Someone
Starts measuring something. It's crawling with black uniforms.
Notes are taken and someone's digging too.
A hand which is raised white, like a faux pas
In a life, strikes every face dumb.
They've found an oil barrel, welded shut.
It's torched open. They bring a body bag –
Clammy, in the garden, Pornschlegel
Wakes. A catnap opens the doors of the dream.
He dabs his forehead. But the trees greet him,
Glasses throw out sparks. He smiles at phlox
And gladioli in the border. He tidies
Himself up in the pressure of the mirror.
He kick-starts his Vespa. He needs to buy an axe.

He was as simple as a carpenter.
He's anything but that now. In the course of events
He was visited in dreams and now he's starting

To believe that mumbo-jumbo of the
Body. His home is draughty, an Aeolian
Harp. The trees he has to cut down,
It breaks his heart. He loves Italian disco.
He says he's an island, la di la. They say
He speaks in metaphors. A man who could be
His brother says: 'He's been unbearable since
Our parents died. He's become unsociable,
An oddball.' He says he has an ever-changing
Effigy. He sings when he's sad.
La di la. La di la di la.

'Who saw me on a snow-white scooter riding
Through the Thursday? The sun was high. The grass
Faded almost to hay beneath its light.
I had no shadow at noon, perhaps because
I was moving fast, but that moment was short-lived.
It seemed withheld from me. The green foliage
Was flashing. The tarmac had a prehistoric
Gleam. The air might have been called almost
Byzantine by someone other than me
Because the blue was filled with a vivid pattern
Of mare's tails and cumulus made and who,
I thought, would read in ordinary things and
Events – the striking of a match, a diabolo
Twirling above a wall, the panicked flutter
Of a coaltit mesmerised by its picture
In a window-pane, although that image
Barely contains life – no parallels here
In weather like this with what's going on in his heart?
It's an almost antique feeling in a period
Just as antique: the depths of summer. The leather
Saddle smelt new. The rubber of the
Tyres whizzed as it touched the roadway. Wish
I could find myself more often like here, *sufficient*
Unto myself, simply shopping. No
Foreshadowing anywhere of inferiority
Or fate. And it showed, I believe: I was
As handsome as Montgomery Clift.

(I imagine people admire me for my hair,
Because it's as white as cocaine. In the sauna,
In department stores, walking through
The park, I've caught people staring, in an
Unguarded moment, as if at the white eye
Of a hypnotist. My hair isn't long and thick:
That's dangerous. I know from experience
That people get entangled in wood, the branches
Of an oak. No. It's very short,
A crew-cut, almost unreal.) With these thoughts
I sliced through the midday. Two minutes
Of happiness can suffice to acquire
A little bit of world in fragile form.
Then the cathedral hove into view like a
Caesura in my reflections. The sun burned
On my arms. My minutes passed by in an instant.
The sound of the scooter was quiet, monotonous. My brother
And his idiosyncrasies were not here.
Day under a bell-jar and acacia
Branches waved after me. I wasn't greeted
By a soul. There've been more festive entries.
Close to the tunnel a glitch in reality threw me:
A young woman in red high heels freed
Herself from the shadow of houses. Her vivacity
A dissonant note in this city of sleep. Her nut-brown
Thighs touched the light. She crossed the street.
Turned towards me, half-way across. Looked at
Me like a cat in a headlamp beam. (Did she want
To shout something, alert me to something, a
Connection, a danger, a resemblance? Was it
This that startled her? Or did I appear
Out of nowhere against the light?) The scooter
Screamed like a maniac. The woman, it seemed,
Couldn't get away from the tarmac. That moment
I felt as soft as the roadway. But even so
I stopped in less than this. Cold rose
From her skin. The gloss on her lips. Her sex was flaunted
Blue in her eyes. Though dazed, she stood there like
A painting. My smile was as hard and smooth as a dildo.'

In years which were perfectly his: his mother,
In a turquoise dress, her neck
Hung round with pearls, walks with him,
Sometimes dragged along by the wind,
Humming along the Sinksenfoor.
Blue is her colour in all its shades.
Her nails, by contrast, scarlet in the
End. Past 'Dr Fuji's Freakshow',
Past 'Will-o-the-Wisp', 'Titine'. And then
Hoisted into the air by a pinion
And he, with mum young for the last
Time, through circles, figures-of-eight,
Arabesques, loops not quite
For mortals, riding the Toboggan
For ever and then look — no hands.

Sent forth at his brother's desire he heads past
The Harmonie. Pornschlegel is seen
Riding where the electricity
Lies bound. Holidays have rehoused the city.
If there are caresses in hallways, in kitchens, in
An atrium, it's out of character:
The heat detracts. *He fell out with his brother*
Over something that got up his nose. He skims
Round the corner, an apparition still light,
Towards the Belgiëlei. There a child
Is walking, a silver heart-shaped balloon in its hand,
Does it follow a similar creed? *The will*
Gave to each his share: the parental home
For brother with son and wife who, let it be said,
Is pretty as a picture but very faithful,
And for Victor Pornschlegel (the notary
Read), i.e. the oldest, he's a guy
Whirring like the sun, but now with a thorn
In his side. How come approach always seems to lead
To delay, *an outbuilding suitable for a single*
Man, with plane-trees around it. He doesn't know
And who has to be somewhere? That driving along
Can act as asylum as long as the heat-wave lasts

And the target is shifting again. *Master of the*
Ruling farm is to have from his brother right
Of way and also right of view, as if he were being
Throttled. To this end he, Victor,
Must fell his old trees. A boy shouts
Something in Yiddish. Another reads a book
From right to left. *'That I contest his right.'*
A new link is looming. *'But what's to be done?'*
He'll hesitate till he's lost, you'll see. *'A kip*
On the sofa. Nibble some figs and bits of cheese,
And later a glass of gin at the kitchen table?'

He turns down the Pelikaanstraat,
Seeking a hardware shop.
His speed is illicit, it seems,
But slowly he feels it drop.
Lethargy seizes the scooter.
What fatal thing is at hand?
The divine machine is lifeless.
He finds no explanation,
For the shadow of Central Station
Seems like the mouth of hell.
Laughter rings like a bell.
The bike to the kerb he pushes,
For the laughing voice he heads,
Past those who trade in time
And refuse that reeks of the grave.
Yonder a glitter he spies.
A boy on the pavement sits,
Whose hair is coaltit-black,
His years are half Pornschlegel's.
One eye's green, one's blue,
As if his soul shines through.
A uniform of glitter
Fits his body tight.
The youngster bids him stop.
'This day is full of the possible,'
Thinks Pornschlegel the man.
On the boy's suitcase he seeëth

The words: '*L'âme des uns*
Jamais n'use de mal'. The sound
Of laughter there, metallic
Now, a doll has appeared
On his hand. What screeching thing
Is this? Already more people
Are watching. 'To live like a prince
Is your wish. You can if you take us
With you. If not, you'll have
To pay. Blood is very
Special juice.' That's
The doll. Not a muscle twitches on the
Face, whence all feeling has fled,
Of the boy ventriloquist, waxen pale.
The doll, however, screams it. In
A trice his brother's voice recognised:
Spiteful and unbending. Victor
Pornschlegel thinks: I'll sort this shit out
Once and for all. The doll to pieces
He smashes, the boy he kicks his head in.

The kid screams to the skies, Pornschlegel hollering
After: 'Only blood will cleanse!' Off
Pornschlegel goes, lickety-split. He's got no
Bloody idea what the little bastard meant.
He thinks it might have been a trick. Before
You know it, you're robbed. But the money still yammers in his
Pocket. On he hurries through streets, through alleys
And arcades. The light turns: he hasn't
Much time to find the shop. A parfumerie,
A grocer's, a barber's, a restaurant. The evening
Heat makes everything smell double. And then,
At a fruit-shop, he sees a melon lying on a trestle,
Hacked in two. The black seeds and the wet
Flesh. Do you have to see its insides? Pornschlegel
Reels. He thinks that someone, as cool as ice,
Is reading his thoughts and plans. Is he being
Followed? He looks behind, now left, now right,
Through alleys, gateways, passages. Tram-rails gleam.

An old man, in shirt-sleeves, trudges along
The pavement like a seedy knight behind
His will-o-the-wisp. Pornschlegel walks past bars,
Cafés, leather-clad boys. He thinks: 'Is desire
Trying to thwart me?' He finds himself in streets
Where red neon, blue neon burns. Suddenly –
He stares to the side - he thinks he recognises
The girl from the afternoon. Azure pumps
And brown thighs, along which her fingers glide.
Her wet tongue makes a promise. Now he sees
Himself reflected in glass. That the light had gone
From his eyes! He runs and runs. Then, at the end
Of an avenue: a hardware store. They've closed.

(epilogue)

He who returns, returns like Hölderlin from the gardens
Of Bordeaux. There, for the first time, he saw
The sea and how the sun baptises its heroes. Again
And again. For everything is return for the one who was touched
By Apollo's hand. Thus Pornschlegel walks the streets,
Disturbed as Hölderlin. It's morning, it's evening. He hasn't
A wife weaving, waiting and unpicking like me.
I seem to remember he wanted what he didn't
Want. The sun wheels high above and in it
His brother, a back, turns and remains a back.
In the streets where Pornschlegel was riding he seemed
To be riding. All parts, of a missing whole.
And then: an axe can work wonders brand-new.
It might be going to rain. And also: a dream,
What do you mean by that? When (days later?)
He wakes, sick to the stomach, he thinks: there's a
Soft and cheerful rain. A roof of leaves
Won't give much shelter. But Pornschlegel stands and stares
At the sun – it's him, as large as life. And the gurgling
In the gutter: this you notice too.
Now it's July and how's life?

Darwin

The reef is alive.
Its own remembering
Anchors a reef to its beginning.

It looks like the palace floor
Of one more Troy
But it's a colony of the sea

In the sea. It must have forgotten
The surrounding ships
And the walkers in themselves.

Never more accurately
Portrayed than by itself
Can a reef's heart still be found –

Scattered in the field, the
Vowels from dozens of sentences.
Your lifespan

Is a hart's horn coral
That hasn't quite
Got going.

People here are few and far between.
On the Beagle it was
In 1836, April,

That Darwin, a wisp of cloud,
Moved over Darwin's diary.
Darwin evaporated,

The reef keeps building the reef.

Anja's Wardrobe 1

Where, caught out, the mirror cracked,
Anja's wardrobe rises black as shoe polish.
With the approval of none of the visitors
It might have been put here one night.
If Anja laces up her little boots, then someone
There goes and does it too, but oh so smugly.
If she puts on a scarf the door
Tangles her. There's not a trace of wood
Left on the wardrobe. It might have white
Sheets, porno mags, cartons of custard inside,
It absorbs things you like and does away with them.
Anja's wardrobe now isn't what a wardrobe was.
Since it appeared mousy-quiet in our lives
They've been split into places. It takes
The world to pieces. Devises a here,
A *there*. Tomorrow morning, unless it's too late,
When Anja's cigarette-end is already glowing,
I'll have to carry it into the dripping garden.
Pour petrol over it, before we
Get caught, Anja and me, in all the kerfuffle
Of Anja's wardrobe.

Anja's Wardrobe 2

So malevolently complete, waxed
-- As if no no-one in the world could smell it --
Anja's wardrobe wants to keep the line of the pillars,
Sycamore, arcades, and how best to eat olives here.

The wardrobe is held together with lies: what lives
Has faded. It's noble to die. I can only go in a
Venetian doctor's mask. The inch-thick wood
A warning in itself: is it planning a spy-hole?

Her wardrobe gleams, but how meekly
Obscene is it on the inside? Anja's wardrobe is
Anja's life. So far, she's stayed
Inside, inside, inside.

Anja's Wardrobe 3

She's so thin, just a wisp of a thing.
Reduced to a Cheshire cat's grin,
Anja, in herself, doesn't exist
That easily. She's a name scratched

In spiky letters on a door.
A nicotine stain on the wash basin.
And she appears in poems:
She's somewhere else in the unfinished

I think myself understood in. There, our conversation
Slaps against the floor, like a skipping-rope.
A change of rhythm is as good as a rest —

This is the only bearable relationship.
Except for the wardrobe, we're all replaceable:
It's a threat to law and order.

The things it'll do not to be a sonnet.

Velázquez: The Portraits of Philip IV

He steps forward, a new order.
In ten portraits
Escaped from the maelstrom.
His allotted patch of light is tight.

Each king fitting inside the next
Like a son. Surrounded by inertia
And a stormy sky. The painter by which
The suspected made itself portrayed —

That this prince wanted to fade away
Each time, as the clouds speed
Over Castile. Only to rise again,
Marshal's staff in hand,

From his chosen silver and brown.

from

Diep in Amerika

(Deep in America)

Translated by
Francis R. Jones

Three Men and the Sea

As long as I'm on the dike
I can be seen from the window
that will only let itself be known
once the man has crashed through it,
for such is thirst for knowledge.

Then someone imagines
that through the churning white of the air
she can hardly make me out to be a man by the lighthouse
or a boot fleeing from the lee of the pier,
the moment she closes the curtains.

Much later my body can be made out on the tarmac,
its position known as contorted,
for then I've stopped being thought of
as wishing I could stand in a flapping, light-blue suit in front of
        the casino,
a fair-haired man the equal of what he can do,
whilst I was about to open a window
which was asking for just that.

In a Drained Bathtub

It's an afternoon for throwing a javelin at the sun
or, in a drained bathtub, hearing yourself beaten by Mahler's
    unworldly strings.

Someone declares that ears by Botticelli
were softer
than drawn by Mantegna.
A photo
shows us
the wonderful huts
as the huts in flames.

You imagine yourself to be a javelin thrower.
Even if people here go crazy
with the echoes, it's good for us
to be absorbed
in the unliteralness of the signs, because things outside
are wild and
everlasting and
empty.

Then the javelin quivers in the field of grass
or rouged lips move along your thigh.

The Return of the Body

Where I am a flower meadow
is missing, even though I'm standing in
a parched flower meadow
with hair blossoming like an orchard
in April.

But whenever I'm cut off
from me by eyes,
like that girl on the bird sofa under a vault of breathlessness,
the body comes
clumsily back and, in desperation
or love
for the kitchen table, lies shuddering on the kitchen table.

Then you think you know it's always there,
even though you're putting your trust in the vacuum
of a dream.

Someone sees all along that the jug, after pouring out
hot water
and being filled with cold water,
breaks in two
and stays broken in two.

Ariel and Jezebel

Who runs under orange skies
along the cinder track and then
runs with Ariel
at ever receding suburbs,
without having left
the order of the liveable.

By the garden wall Jezebel stops,
recoiling two steps backward.
So far
she only knows him from the sighs
I heave at the sound of his name.

But she would let
her boyish body be smeared with honey by countless hands
to call Ariel
upon her, in a swarm of bees.

In the meantime
he remains in the patchy memory
of the heat of a day which refuses to exist,
except in the sprinting
of someone
who doesn't like sprinting.

Lynx Time

Only after the dream-time
does a summer's day dawn on me
out of the alleged sharpness
from which others wish themselves a refuge that doesn't exist as such.

Elsewhere the crystal of a chandelier,
crashing down amidst
what could have been
the life and soul of a party,
seeks another destination.

Just as lying awake at night turns
over and over whilst listening
for a car which doesn't swish
along a rain-wet street.

Then, scarcely touched
by dazzle, lynx comes
snorting through summer,
point-eared,
on the run
and tries, with bloody paws,
to seek safety on what is called a candelabra cactus

outside the shade.

from

Hartswederwaren

(Happenings of the Heart)

Translated by
John Irons and Francis R. Jones

The Never Inviolate

Heart, if only you were there,
an approachable character in
the Eurostar beneath the North Sea, her icy
masses of water merging in tints of green
signifying a shifting context or the intractability
of community (in the form of lunch, paddle fest
or mutual trust) that constantly reaches past itself;
           chess companion
though I do not play chess;
           cold ear, still unknown
against which my lips rest;
           neck-brace; credit line.

But you are only known,
heart, in the reaches beyond my doctrinal
gloom, fluorescent volcanic ash
which, toxically descending, covers tables and chairs
and fashions us untenably
for the day
that no longer recognises us.

Almost the heart
eluded me in its legacy
a mass grave of faces, moss-covered
tree trunks in the Soignes forests carved through with love,
chalk lines, receding blood, emblems
obscured
by speaking of them,
and only beating in this obscurity,
a description of a landscape,
carte du coeur, of the never inviolate that binds
in which outgrowths
of its history were settled.

Translation: JI

The Body In Amherst

Heart, in Dickinson
you are a gift, surpassing
by far my thissing here, as a giving
in the making, a payment
that decays in hands
covered with flesh flies
like offal from another world,
exceeding by far, a caress
for a tongue like honey
from clover in 1858
or an apricot
left to soak in a bowl
of water that goes on quivering,
supposing the body in Amherst
belongs to love.

Full of flesh you feed
the spirit,

There chimes the bell
in Amherst, a heart
pumping beneath a crinoline

It is the bell
that rings the death knell
over the words that evaporate like ether
in case
her grammatised body
has no other heart than her restitched book-work,
staked out like a white-painted fence
round a house with veranda that is on fire

like a cunt without a name
in an age without women

Translation: JI

From The Transient

Heart, I can consider you in generous terms

of imagery to prove your transferable

nature, your utility, Generator,
for the reclamation of unreclaimed land;
reservoir for the felt

or what in touch with our mortality
emits signals in biochemistry.

As a cistern for the emotions,
that which moves us, I could incorporate
you in the rhetoric
of the preceding, but, as rhetoric,
the preceding has already done so
and as such incorporated me, so that I
address myself from the transient in you
that reinvents me in what you do to me

Translation: JI

Injury To The Heart

a)

We never get used to it, for it falls
into language and spreads like a disease, that loads and appears
to be loaded history. A single chair greets the idea of sitting, fixed
in its form through use. In photographs all chairs that ever were
rouse panoramic views that makes you piss your pants for joy.

The first morning drags blackly behind us **then** like the trail of
blood from folded-up ox-hide, over a French pavement where the
slaughtering wails like endlessly slammed steel that was reforged
into a gate.

'And innocence? The bare beginning?'

Take the Turin shroud. Apart from the saturated cloth, it is
the trace of a story, poured from the casting mould of ideology,
topped up perhaps with a discourse on DNA and carbonisation.

Each word an abattoir.

That is how the heart *became*

what we call *our* heart, since it plays havoc in each one of us.

Empty it and drenched with blood a storm rages through the
heavens.

Eat it and take part in the transfiguration.

At times this organ is a friendly heart. A pale, glossy tuber on
the window sill touched by the light like the stinking breath of a
prince.

Isn't your view of the world the world filled by the body
(sprouting like a nightshade in the sun) that reaches for the world
with purple claws, hankering for love, an act of intimacy?

What beats in me goes on beating in you.

Who does not cherish this organ
for its modesty and the purification of its seizures?

Guillaume de Guardestaing and
Guillaume de Roussillon,
butcherer and rival.

Philostratos, cast down by love.

In history, heart, you are a prey to migration that you
contradict in what people claimed you to be.

I see no one who knows you licking their lips with glee.
So deadly wide the world's stage –
hazy heart
in a hazy age.

b)

A load of crap is said about you, heart,
empty signifier,

good-natured twit, though homeless in the cardboard box of the
twentieth century, with melting ice-caps, algae in the Adriatic and
angels living in radiation measurable in becquerels.

Old-fashioned heart, ousted
by microprocessors that only generate
you as a binary *ars combinatoria*,
although that makes bliss
emerge in me as wimpish fear –
or with the fibre-optic camera
travelled through on a Saturday night
in Asimov's dream and the live ops on national TV,

swapped for the dilated arse
in its unfathomable emblematics, contemporary,

where else have you sailed off course than in sailing?

Translation: JI

Heart, *you piece of shit,*

Who imagined seeing you appear
in all your glory
as the gold-leaf covered seat
of unattainable love
in a throne room
at the end of a stuccoed passage,
adorned with rocaille and cut-glass mirrors,
is now wading through
the putrid pulp of the abattoir.

You are a disease that has become flesh.
A stinking gag in the mouth.
The shit from the guts
of a breed that stuffs the shit from its own guts
because that is all it has to stuff.

Our thoughts go out to you
who reels around inside us like the name of an other
for whom one pours oneself
in the passive voice and fades
into a sore spot that wavers
between manual healing and amputation

and we carry you in us,
the glory the stars
a heavenly throne a piece of shit
cherished as a dream
of a world that feeds us so we
can cherish the dream

Translation: JI

Boogie Man

Heart, the market square
is slashed with hail and swamped with *floodlight*.
In the *Café du Commerce*
the waiters roam around orphaned
in someone's play or phone,
now you feel the situation's fraught, their dealers
and the whole city falls ill.

For an instant it happens that you,
as if put through the wringer,
have eyes on stalks,
thundering like a cartoon, howling
in the sirens of Dresden,
unverfroren, an accomplished defence lawyer,
inedible at mass

For there she sits smoking beneath her red hair
vacant as the world in the jewishness of her first name,
and to begin with each gesture
is a happening that makes you clatter like a stork
in a documentary or natural reserve

But there she sits
and she cannot hear your *boogie*.

It is no bed of roses.
When she kisses
the secret story of the heart
kisses the slapstick of everyday

Translation: JI

In Hospital

Bared heart, let yourself be dragged, gasping for breath,
through the mire,
cold fledgling on the satin of a cushion
blue as the dripping wound
of Amfortas,

where the darkness yawns, deep
in a gullet, nil between lungs,
reamed with stinking russula,
a sphincter which no longer shuts.

All that I am

is dragged round with this

given respiration under the lights
of a hospital
called love –

yes, that's what we believe.

Translation: FRJ

Still Smouldering Love

Above the
(marble in the festive season)
folded fabric of her
heart-into-soul-turning dress
surging as ebb tide, blood
that floods outwards,
fat and hunger in a tunic
of flesh fallen from its own province
into a mineral shape, there stands
in the relative simplicity of its pose

an angel, taking up its post
in the composite space of the baroque,
ruled by a principle
that was tapped from us
by reason in the sleep of
reason: chaos
as the jubilant foliage
of a deciduous wood forever external to our sweat
and the persistent crisis that makes believing impossible for us
as we hover lifelong on a speechless pavement
in a coma in the city
that implements us
in the speaking that others do for us

and prepared to throw a bridge
between our body, logged
onto the *collapsing*,
and the absence to that body
that seems to be expressed in this eclipse,
this retching of a thing
to which there is no end

by means of a silver arrow with your name on it
representing the God that strikes

dumbfounded,
known to himself as
the one perforating you with incineration

the ashes of our

like our own mortal remains

still smouldering

love, heart,

and she does it,

it happens

it is the

singing of a superstring

All Blood (from 'Blood's Triptych')

The day begins, because a day begins
and it is blood from a bleeding heart
with which the day begins

Someone looks around on a wet platform
and there is blood everywhere
coursing through people's faces,
clouding as steam on a train window, in the mediocrity
of our violins, that echoes
like wailing through the dark passages

The floor of the abattoir, a spinning wheel, Dahmer's
bath tub – the gutter A silhouette on the road
cannot contain all that blood

But his day begins and it is only this:
he bleeds out of bed, bleeds to the bathroom,
bleeds into his clothes, the blackest thoughts
they bleed black out of his nose,
he stands bleeding between two strips of the zebra crossing
while the ground bleeds away beneath him
and what then in the presence of car drivers
bleeds out of him into view

bleeds all imagination

Translation: JI

Fables Of The Sacred Heart

1)

Those were days of mountain cycling. Up hill and down dale. There was an enormous hunger for more and as long as, smelling of groaning resin, they block a view of the immaculate summit, the pine trees epitomise this desire only too well: above the tree line, there you feel free.

Stumbling along a rocky path Jesus
kept on treading on the hem of his robe.

He had missed the refreshment stations. He was the only cyclist on foot. The wind tore his garments to rags. Lightning roamed through his hair. We had all cycled off
in different directions.

When he reached the bare, snow-covered summit, Jesus turned his head in bewilderment. No homestead. No last burrow of emotions. No powerful, ascetic birds. Never had anyone disappointed him more than Rilke.

At that moment, Jesus saw his Father's pearly whites
flash in the valley. In some sort of message His dentures formed
the words 'YOU SUCK'.

As dispossessed as the state of his calling,
Jesus then pulled two ribs apart in the white marble
of his glorious figure and, as the blood gushed from his ribcage like
a mudslide razing a mountain village, displayed his Sacred Heart
to a nation watching TV.

We saw the grit and determination of a kid who's spent a life
crawling through sewers.

This was no Jesus. This wasn't the Corcovado Jesus. Not the Dear Lord who Speaks to Us.

This was a mountain bursting out of its being.

2)

The woods were a violent prey to turmoil. Jesus led the way,
a devouring fire. The gravity of his brow. The velocity of his
footwear. His breath surged like a rocket through time. He oracled
freely,
had it all chronicled
though in his role
as the One that Is to Come
he was virtually
incomprehensible: someone had tampered with his food, his
blood-sugar level.

A thick cloud spread out over the swimming pool
and scattered soot into the skies.
Thus centuries combined into an illegible sign. Someone saw a
plane crashing. A murmuring woman sank down by a bush. We
feared a sandstorm or a billboard collapsing and perhaps that huge
alien object was a swimmer who, arms flailing,
leapt from a diving tower
in the following town.

Sometimes the world formulates
an answer
in the form of an excrement
that drives the blood from our pores.

In Jesus too no end to that blackness was granted.

Although he was the One Coming, he was also the One Going

whereupon he curdled and a rent appeared in the outgrowth.

At that moment His Heart slipped out
between shirt buttons
and zigzagged away, into the skies.

'Be all,' so said our saviour
'like this spaceship, in its dying,
with seven burning humans on board. So must your heart be: an
engine that rattles and hums in the sleep of death.'

But all that we saw was slobber
on his shirt.

3)

At that time Jesus lived in the heart of Anna of Jesus, the giggling
of Myriam or the flower-print dresses of Pipilotti Rist. Dead-still
he lay in his bed. His sleep was as deep as the Marianas trench.
White was the room, with a window (bricked-up), a door (nailed-
up), a bed (live with electricity) and a toilet (filled with concrete).
The camera whirred. Outside time roared past
like light darts from nova to nova.

Knowledge doubles, and yes: 'We have a jesus.'
Humanity, a zoological given.
Armenia. Kampuchea. Rwanda.
Byzantinism, rococo, pensiero debole.
We plough and plough the shit of being.

Invisible flames licked Jesus' toes and during these two thousand
years his heart, with the relentlessness of a stalactite --
in a Holy Crack of the dark --
had beat but once.

4)

In Vienna Jesus lodged
next to the baritone and the soprano. The baritone crapped and
the soprano let her hair down in scales that waltzed like wisteria
through the blossoming spring, but for Jesus all that was a razzia,
a Chinese dragon in the streets, a fuse hissing through the world at
lightning speed, an assault on his being and the emptiness of which
it consisted. 'Eloï, Eloï,' he shouted down the phone, '*don't fuck
with me.*' But Dad was not there and Jesus pretty peeved.

'Every distraction is a demon,' Jesus shouted, with flaring nostrils,
whereupon he drove his wrath
through the boarding house like a clean-up team.

That evening he was sitting dazedly in the Oper,
when it transpired
that during the interval his Sacred Heart
in the simplicity of its unfolding
became a colourful spectacle — with a lyrical podium, innumerable
voice modulations, a text stolen from Fabre
and a packed hall —
and in Vienna murder and pillage was rife.

5)

Each day has enough in its own suffering and therefore Baselitz
painted *rechts und links eine Kirche* (oil on canvas, '87). His blue
was the background for the blond of a doll that became flesh and
depicted the urge to .... *(fill in for yourself)*.

Jesus too hadn't got a clue.
He was having a bad trip.
It seemed to him that he was looking at the world without a
decoder.
At around Frankfurt he left the Bundesbahn
and in his stylish suit he could have
stepped out of *Corporate Wars*. The DAX pumped capital through
the world and generated a heat
like that of a particle accelerator,
but Jesus was in the wrong skin.
His teeth chattered as through struck by the hand of God
at the sight of the *Wilden*, he was all
of a sweat, went off in search of the white, cooling porcelain
of a bathroom,
addressed an urgent word
unto himself
and shit his soul out.

The Sacred Heart
ascended
in a feast of sound and vision.

6)

In search of the greatest delicacy of all history, Etienne Binet, a
Jesuit with the gaze of Robespierre, made a list of titbits in *Des
attraits tout puissants de l'amour de JESUS-CHRIST* (1631).

It turned out to be a historical hit parade:
- the pearl that Cleopatra swallowed with a gulp of wine
  vinegar
- the phoenix, devoured by a greedy emperor as an evening
  meal
- the ashes of Mausoleus, mixed with wine in a golden goblet
  and drunk by his wife Artemisia
- the apple, bitten by Adam
- the manna, bread of heaven and great pleasure of the angels.

But all this is merely a figure of speech,
Binet says, a fable
that depicts the flesh of love
given to us by Jesus
in the over-abundance of his mercy.

Should we not call that flesh a fleshy growth
or a blackhead in the face of God
that like a solar flare is being squeezed into nothingness?

Or perhaps it is
a gobbet of phlegm like a dripping by Pollock
that is licked out of the wash basin by man,
obsessed as he is with his own decomposition.

7)

It was the summer of the bandana and Jesus joined in the trend.
The Man of Sorrows was written off. He wanted to rid himself of
that hairshirt.
'*Life's a beach*,' he said calmly, resolutely.
'As of today I am the Guy
who represents the Cool of the West.'
He cracked his knuckles and grabbed his Gucci.

'Piss mug.'
'Dick wad.'
'Filthy faggot.'

Voices rose out of the floor. The walls were standing blood. The
crystal of the chandelier quivered. Someone laughed so loud that
Jesus thought of a clyster.
Was this the arrival of *jouissance*,
unimaginable psychotic pleasure,
or had the son of man fallen prey to semiotic confusion?

'Jacaranda.'
'Huhediblu.'
'Bwana Kitoko.'

The local signs did not affect his soul. 'But ladies,' Jesus said, while
sniffing at panties that had been sent to him through the post, 'I
am your redeemer. Your rose water and eye bath. The stiff state of
your clit.'

Seriously concerned
about his level of Cool
Jesus went out on the balcony and displayed *(yet again)*
his heart to the Belgian people.

Everything that bled, spurted and moved there
was maggots
in the form of a bird's carcass.
Deboned.
Held in gelatine.

8)

A little later, when clouds gathered and stars imploded, Jesus reached a property by the name of Gethsemane. In solitude, he sank down and took a hand-mirror out of his backpack. He spoke with a girl's voice to the steamed-up image: 'I am a field of Whitsun flowers. The wet snout of an otter. The swish of silken slippers. The fingertips with which Chopin strokes his piano. The load of white lilies your lover dumped on your doorstep. The aubergine that melts on the tongue. Your voice thick with tears. The pale face of a German dancer at the hour of dawn. The leveret of her belly. The trotting of a horse. The smile of the newscaster. White light. White heat. The rush of the roller coaster. The bungee jump. The vision that dawns during the crash that no one survives. The mountain peak that makes you giddy with joy. The hand that leads you through this area where you have no business to be. Even more: I am the merry madcap. The hissing butter. The scent of honey. A word of love. Jan Hoet. Tears of joy. A vineyard in blossom. The wit of Jan Hoet. A day in the country. The dew on the grass. The flowers on Mother's Day. The subtlety of Jan Hoet. The weather simply a dream. A sight for sore eyes. A wonderful sunset. Their bodies as seeds. No more war. Our all for Flanders. The Diamond Awards. The A and the Z. The DIY farmstead. A cloudless sky. Limes' fragrance bitter-sweet. Girls' lips that softly meet.

And that was completely unnecessary.
There was not a soul that heard this.

Besides, we yearned for the wound that bears, the surf, the dike when it bursts, the cream that curdles, high fever, the dirt that creeps out from under our nails, the fat that ruins pale thighs, the stone in the cherry, the urge, screeching brakes, the spewing, dire emergency, the goal that is no goal, menacing clouds, desire when it does not quite formulate itself, the well-nigh, the approximate, the *ing-form* and the nevertheless.

9)

It was time.
The Day of the Second Coming.

Jesus gazed at the firmament
that took on the colour of nitroglycerine.
He spat in slow on the ground
and from the chrome-and-dividivi-tanned
skin of his body
now taken up into the heavens
the Sacred Heart descended on the world.

Was this the *beau Dieu* from the portal at Chartres?
The triumphant heart
that tramples snakes, lions and dragons underfoot?
The pantokrator? A child with grape, bird, nimbus?
It resembled a unicorn but appeared to be a piranha.
A handful of dough scooped from the trough of his father.
It was a woman, with Oliver Hardy's smile

and while we walked through the gardens of Notre Dame,
there was much wailing, pissing and shoving.

But the game was worth the candle

for now the Sacred Heart is amongst us,
the world has been shifted one millimetre and

that

makes all the difference

Translation: JI

Looking At Mountains

When the Swiss evening falls,
backlit behind the billowing white of curtains
the mountain's watching.

Its stare is the mucus
in the heart of things
that hounds us onward, hunted heart.

It's a swish
of granite
shifting slyly through our thoughts.

It lives in a hand
casting itself like shadow
across the bent back of a smiling man
who's tucking his kids in bed or, late at his drawing board,
drafting another facade of the world.

If you've ever looked at a mountain,
the mountains will always be looking back,
even if it's a wisp of mist,
the sound of a cowbell, the scree
that splits our attention in the moraine.

Translation: FRJ

The Heart's Heart

It's the heart's heart: heart attack,
when matter hangs and crashes, shot
through with black tissue, by which
the body declares itself, to the house and
its red-blooded habits or the walk
by the freezing reservoir,
to be sunken into its state of flesh,

to be a muscle deserted by being so.

In its blue, the core of its collapse,
the heart is like a beast that, in clammy
exile from oxygen
to the limits of its anatomy,
is more than itself when dying
and thus interwoven with the poem –
which, attack after attack,
presents itself to the passing and so
again and again,

as death strikes the writing,

destroys its part of the world.

Translation: FRJ

from

De wind uit het elders.
In praise of Barnett Newman

The Wind from Elsewhere.
In Praise of Barnett Newman

Translated by John Irons

2)

Good morning, Barnett Newman.
Have you slept well?
Was your bed soft enough and did the babbling brook
of our heating system
not keep you from a good night's rest?
Last night was icy and in the moonlight the landscape
manifested itself as extraterrestrial.
Wasn't the return journey tiring?
There are clean towels for you in the shower.
We have bought you some new shirts.
You can borrow my uncle's bow tie.
Should you presently wish to take a walk, I would warn you
that the footpaths in this country are narrow, the houses ugly,
the food rich though unreliable.
The world has become a bit more affluent
since your death in 1970, but people still die as before: they
are pitched into mass graves or the sea or into cesspools. One
incinerates them in cars, lets them choke in their own puke, slits
them open and takes out some of their guts, pours hydrochloric
acid on their eyes and smashes their heads to pulp, amputates
hands and legs, dissolves them in caustic soda and pours the slush
through the waste pipe.
Give man what he deserves, I'd say
and the arts?
For Baudrillard art has evaporated
into the ecstasy
of value (bank accounts, fetishes
in shop windows), while it is basically form (he says)
and transformation
of form into form and as such indestructible
and valueless (*seule la forme peut annuler la valeur*),
and an unemphatic blossoming outgrowth of matter
and that too your work proffers us.

Your heart has been repaired.
Let us do some stretch-and-bend exercises at the open window
together. The rollers and brushes are ready and waiting.

The way you are standing there
in the garden that is cast in twilight
you look like a door ajar, the pupil of a cat
contracting in the light, facing a swirling whirlpool,
a hair-crack in the bone of the world,
a gasp of breath evaporating in the cold
and I thank you for that

3)

Barnett Newman, blissfully moustachioed,
plasmically unavoidable,
baldly irritable in 1951
in the photo with Pollock, Rothko, Still and Motherwell,
Thoreau fan, attracted by the Zimzum,
that insane space,
devoid of God, no flowers for you
(no wooden buckets or landscapes
in the surrealist style)

who brought the picture out of balance,
the symmetry grounded in the human figure,
and brushed a phosphorescent
stroke named
after tearing fabric, the onomatopoeic
cleaving of air by singsinging glass,
that worked loose a field of colour out of
the seeable,
denying us what we know

There is a ray of seething light
lead that
plummets down its vertical and then the body

that upright,

organises the division
of space:
the extreme minimum
opposite the extreme maximum

6) Vir heroicus sublimis

Who art in paintings,
in us a sombre panorama
was constructed,
with traffic arteries, beaches, chemical ground,
cisterns, endlessly
shunting trains in underground stations
lit up day and night
from the inside by electronics,
in which waves that people call muzak
diffusely involve the ceiling light and I think of other things
for everything is shattered, at one go,
and we are standing in the blood-curdling gaze
of the red that thickens into chaos.

Sighing, cautiously
in rural Bronx,
out of piano lessons
and Hebrew in a child
out of the thought of Spinoza and Kropotkin
a man rises up,
a small man in America
in search of a subject
for painting,

a subject, no decorative form

à la Malevich, à la Mondrian

Writing, so as to have a beginning

Man in perspective

No argument needed

11) A photo

The apparition of the blue
This is the birth of the self into the world
or Barnett Newman
with an unknown woman, in front of the Cathedra in 1958

'Do you see nothing there,' Hamlet asks

It is a man a gazer
in front of a gaping deep gazing back
at the mercy of
the seeable that sees
sucked up by a wall of colour,
less real than his shadow
which the flash casts
onto the blue reduced
to the many shades of grey

The canvas as ectoplasm
kneading itself into its own onlookers

We only see the object
when it has looked at us first.
Roquentin, stared at by a tree root
Bacon, eye to eye with the carcass
Meursault, observed by the nails in his mother's coffin
Newman, seen
through the folds of God's mantel that fills the tabernacle

No one saw, from this close,
a firmament producing its own light

While this man, this woman
are disappearing into their back
in a dingy kitchen in March
a woman is ironing

That is what one does in a spare moment

from
Zapruder Stress

Zapruder Stress

Translated by John Irons

Soon at a cinema near you

1) The *sequel*

This is where
The story ends. In his Mustang
the bomb Expert Kisses the girl
(*zoom in, dolly back*) And yes, they fuck
like rabbits, living hard & long,
But under the bed the ice-pick

Lurks Bloodlust

in person, Who looks out from the screen,
and In his immaculate white uniform he enters and enters
the factory, Already from afar
In his male seriousness, In the shiny, restrained sex
of his suit. The tension of his cap
Represents the power
of his pectorals *(red)*. Everyone is thinking
of his greasy, well-oiled Thing
He now carries his girl
Outside, over the threshold
(*inspiring music*)

Resistance has been overcome
No doubt a friend had to lose his life,
en route We could
wander around among decors on fire,
with such Dialogues as: 'We've gotta get the hell outa here'
'We'll never get out of this alive'
And: 'Oh, my God, they've shot my husband.
I love you, Jack.'

At a certain moment you have to be open to Joy
But on the terrace *(red)* Of his beach house he is brooding
Behind sun glasses in which the surf rolls and
Foams On a sequel

I admit: the Pacific was never so peaceful,
On the beach, wide and empty as a studio,
I, My thumbs
tucked into my belt, stood
looking at how my being, characterised
by sheer prostration – or no, by
eyes covered with white film –
began to
get cold feet

While in the mountains a pod is being discovered

(From: *The Fucked-Up Egg-Shaped Magenta-Streaked Chromium
Fantasy Machine Going Boom In The Night*)

2) The remake

It all began *(red)*

On a Thursday. an Autumn day,

a day on which
autumn made its entry and entering
was depicted In the telling black&white Of a gust of wind:
seed, spores
that breezed in from the Distance,
a balmy shower as proof
that nature takes her course And music
that heralds danger. On a swing in the park
Sits, in a soutane
that burdens the heart with its Flapping,
a priest

about whom people wonder if it could be Robert Duvall,
with his Dramatic skull

angularly lit, or Jason Miller,
with shaven head, to whack
the demons out of your randy,
pissing flesh

Shadows always *do*
it, interfere
with the emotional balance, but priests are just as effective,
a black, archaic cipher that embodies 'the seriousness of the situation',
the indication
that a majestic evil has arisen
in the world

but what, in god's name,
are those sun-tanned Leather things in the boot,
On the billiard table, foaming like a corpse
in the mud bath?
Your uncle is not your uncle any longer

Everyone suspect

Oh, how it churns and sputters and swells and pukes

especially if you forget to look

(and us just Driving and washing windows)

(and what secret plans

does Leonard Nimoy have?)

But the danger returns unexpectedly

They arrive at the factory

The skirmishes (helicopters, tunnels) indicate the extent of the
ordeal: a certain, painless end for all except one, revealed
in the bestial darkness of a throat in the final shot
the exit
for each one of us

Where first there was no scream
there is a scream now,

that which *(red)*
in you is More than you,

but that was the clue of it All

Only *she who one loves most* normally ends up infected, perhaps
because her love is not strong enough; she is Not of his flesh; her
trust, her white blouse crumpled; in the shoes with which she
stumbles out of her flight into view, awaits exhaustion. Out of her
feverish blush sleep, in an unguarded moment, spreads out
murmuring as desire without being desire
through her vascular system,
so that *(They)*

can suck Themselves From one film

into the other

Always the same song

What kind of adventure have I now
embarked upon

3) The home movie

The truth of things
lies in their exaggeration.
The panic of the midday hour
The neo-classicism of the columns
from the pergolas Sucked off by the Texan metaphysics
of space – more Closely shaved
could the lawn of the Plaza
scarcely be, with here And there
a woman dipped in Red, a man with umbrella
in the dog-light
of the black, high sun, the *black dog man*

behind the November sign
Of the freeway
The Abundance

of the whiter than white
You cannot Know
where something is
and What its speed is at that point.

Only the spear that
Wounds can sear
the wound

I was standing on a concrete block
close to the bridge, mainly
casting shadow, while his petit-bourgeois wife,
in the pink shroud of her Chanel,
bent over him and Someone dies,
in frame 313,
where the stench of philoctetes
is whipped
out of the Bowl
like a scarlet flower-cloud, and francis Bacon
mixes her Suit

through jack's flesh
and his hair through her mouth,
while He leaves his place Behind, that survives him
and is unassailable
by someone else, after which,
almost unnoticed thick flesh and cold flesh
slowly starts to cover the Epoch,

There was a tailor
with a Bell & Wesson Zoomatic,
who did not perceive anything. but Filmed.

(Exhibit 51 photographed
Next to a colour display card from the National Archives)

(Shooting ratio 1:1)

Charles Brehm	.... Himself (onlooker, with son)
Howard Brennan	.... Himself (onlooker) (unconfirmed)
Bobby Hargis	.... Himself (policeman, on motorcycle)
Jean Hill	.... Herself (onlooker, in red coat)

4) The screen version

a

(red)

(water)

(breaking glass)

raincoat

a ball in the pond

a slide in which blood wells up

What compels a person
to Venice, especially in a hopeless burberry?
Restoration, a squall of pigeons, the water
in sloshing cellars,

The city is in many heads
It seems to have asked for it, although its motives are unclear, as are
its methods

Possibly its organisation of water is asking
for people wanting
to die or the foretaste of it

Take this father
gasping, howling
kneeling in a pond with his dead child In his arms
a powerful pose of Donald Sutherland for distress
in which the city announces itself and the book,
dear viewer, destroyed the child
with meningitis

If only you were washed over
with that feeling of the unfathomable that rises out of
Daphne du Maurier like a flight of raven-black

feathers, satisfying some ancient,
neurotic need or other

or A Long knife
that pierces the skin, the resistance of an unpeeled
tomato

Not every character understands that
the future
bleeds among Present things

a gondola, with women in mourning garments,

a man blinded with grief

a red scarf, the burden
of a dead child

who trips through the dark on tiny feet?

Is the moustachioed commissioner
all part of the plot?

al-jebr, the putting-together of fragments

In the slightest
gesture lurks the fatal mechanics
of the outcome

And then we see the face of

(fate)

No! Don't do it!
Don't look

Before it's too late

and after

5) The costume film

The marchioness left

her castle, at
five o'clock, Bored, Talented
and rich ten minutes Later

her tongue twirls
round his *boules d'amour*

The count butters his bread in the sun

wigs, A duel,
intrigues.
A fine role for John Malkovitch
'A vos mouchoirs!'

Though she believes in God and virtue and the sacredness
of marriage,
her cunt foams
with Complex, moral ambivalences

The marchioness falls

victim, for that's the way it goes, Handed over,
with sores or consumption, to an illness,
the external signs

Of her moral depravity

and all of those while morning announces itself as a shabby
servant and the war
breaks out in tumbling plaster

What a Pity that your passion has bereft you of Your senses

You would like to believe it true

The captain or the drummer or the count
exhausts himself

that may be expected of him

in gestures, powdered wigs, with letters
sealed with Sealing wax and dirty text that he hisses at her while the white
of her tits trembles as a sign of lewdness
sauced With fear

The marchioness: a peal of laughter in the coach house

The marchioness: throwing the balcony doors wide and violently open

The marchioness: blushing at the picnic

First a polite greeting, but then,
as the dawn rises, the dispute

is settled with rapiers

(swiftness of action, change of tempo)

The marchioness left her castle

The sun was low on the horizon

All of it the fault of the *passé simple*

Zapruder Stress

Almost

nobody comes by here,
someone said in the plunging
from the 42nd
to street level (*breathe deeply*)

yet it has all the signs
of a mainstay –
a rust- and seaweed-covered
wreck of the real, lopsided in sewer water

about which no one knows

how deadly it is, even from the wellstone
representing coolness when the day is hottest
in which the one undertow
moves against the other
like a disaster (*replay*)
we know so that there is no end to it –
for that is what we would wish

negligence
of lust

you and the illuminated state
of your sleep, glowing
with expectation where none is, in a drifting off
of escapades and what really matters
beneath the trajectory of satellites,
temporary
instability – oh
the fucked-up beauty in cibachromes
of Tokyo
in the sun according to David Byrne

Just let me first
open that tin of peas. The pleasures

of defenestration
according to rem sleep

The world and its apparitions
In its apparitions
the world, hello
world hello apparitions

Was that the agreement?

Almost

your heart overflows:
in Tokyo, where the Japanese
(inhabitants of Japan)
as a rule get stuck *(under furniture)*
and die during an earthquake Shigeru Ban built
a housing project
designed to withstand earthquakes
(Statement of public benefit)

It is a reassurance like 'This evening
our sorrows will have an end'
or 'Shall I soap your back?' or
'A woman – what's
that?' or 'In the market
there's no room for power, only
for daily elections'
(Applause from all benches)

Green light
above Baghdad. You and your
expectations. Your commercial spirit
and contact skills. It's getting
dirtier all the time. The sun has disappeared.
Nice photo collection
of Pol Pot. Did you say something? Oh no,
it's happening again. This capsule *is* an emergency system.
You want a fuckin' medal for that? Too late
is bad luck
and smarter don't help. Oops,
sorry about your orange juice.
In its stubbornness
a wasp as a pastiche
of a charming wasp. *(Now really?)*
Is this the tremor of the Continental shelf?
Here comes the Big One
(Almost –
The last to leave turns off the light.
But where is the switch?

Almost

I let it be known

someone washed ashore in his
statements – a declared hereafter, what a scream, destroyed
walls, the nine, strawberries smeared open, until today a pier support,
planed smooth, peat bog to peat bog, the mobile city,
flashing skies, of the visor, a lopsided jaw, for the self-timer,
for that's how I know how to find you, we all burn up – but does she
know what she means?

Articulated it enters
the pure apostatic
and who said anything about aversion
or fulfilment?

Sometimes I see an enormous mudslide and I think:
time to go.

Is wood flight still possible?
(National Geographic)

Is the world full
of married men?
(Jackie Collins)

I dread it like a mountain
like a mountain am I
I'm gone on it

Almost

off stroke

for how to begin
with this minimal
sacrifice, a fasting of the spirit —

tangible
as a measure —
so he would do everything for you?

is that clear enough?
(*stand up*)

Our recollections like
corrupt versions of a text
(*sit down*) which itself is devolved
recollection
minus slides, super 8, commercial video,
flames flaring from the paper.

You're in fits.

Today we should have come *home*.

The catastrophe is (*stand up*)
what makes our day:
blaring engines,
kerosene vapours, mould
in the garbage, a ferry
that sinks,
(*sit down*) but where
is the Tanganyika Lake?
(*All together now:*

Almost

Everybody knew
that I would back down. Continuity,
I give you that. I said,
that milk's already turned sour.
Dave, I motioned, I've
lost my marbles.
You've only one chance left.
Someone's practising the piano,
swinging the salad colander.
(Oh yes, on this floor Katz
lives gloriously) There's now so little time
that at any moment you will see your hand
change into, well, coagulating
egg-white, released for a moment
from the urge to focus,
this cultural neurosis,
in which we are bathed
and bathe, with an aura
gilt and formal as Europe
though disconcerted, almost moved to tears,
you see how John Kelly and Janice Licalsi
embrace in the dimming
of light by jalousies
and whispering, heavy players
in the code of intimacy
(by which hope installs itself
that, against the background
of the city as meaningless
in its materials, products,
cashflow, hedonism, structure,
John and Janice
by means of their erotic involvement
lead the social fabric
in this type of inevitable metaphorics
like a 'hand in glove'
(apparently people have the acquired need

to mark their cultural identity
in territorial terms
by organising their local
community, getting
a grip on their workplace and domicile,
discovering love, lust and happiness
time and again in the abstraction
of this new, historical landscape with the danger
that the parameters
of their 'specific identity',
which has to be loaded with meaning again
by the concept of 'place',
become precisely impossible to communicate
to the other tribes,
true outsiders, in
the same boat, let's say)
so that the random
(oh, this *coup de dés*
we usually live with)
is framed with an eye to
that subjugation from which we,
whichever way you look at it,
derive a minimal density
so that I can look you in the eye
(with as Levinas says: ethics
as the first philosophy)
be it on the basis of the maxim
'Thou shalt not kill'
transgressible, though restricted
by that other frame
we call law and even so?)
although — on this set —
this erotic incident is not able to be
anything more than an allegory,
slapping against the quay of its own impossible
allegoresis (or — to
draw from the informal register —
a fart in a bottle)

and although those people over there
insist that it should be Schoenberg,
Ligeti or, at least, Shostakovitch
(is that how you spell it?), Phil Glass, Wim Mertens even,
it's Diana Ross, Kylie Minogue and Rob de Nijs
who make the bigtime.
There is no more fearful heart
than mine.
Thanks to the day you want to live.
There's the door.
Use it.
Groovy

Meanwhile, on the set of NYPD Blue...

Almost

we were wrapped up
in our representations,
unnoticed forms
of sentiment

and subjection and our patience
went
there
went our patience

broached during
the barbecue and
lost again, no one knows
how to protect you
from the least that we lack –
a shower, tampon, spare wheel –
one sees how you get in

The world after
poetry,
on the other side of the street

countless ruins,
dreamwork
as the enjoyment
of its own impossibility,
no snow, order
over the tumult of the city, human nature
almost
a document as remains of the fever
that we
can be
oh no

if only I was

Wwwhhhooossshh
(The Opera Ain't Over Till the Fat Lady Sings)

Translated by Willem Groenewegen

"Fame requires every kind of excess. I mean true fame, a devouring neon, not the somber renown of waning statesmen or chinless kings. I mean long journeys across grey space. I mean danger, the edge of every void, the circumstance of one man imparting an erotic terror to the dreams of the republic. Understand the man who must inhabit these extreme regions, monstrous and vulval, damp with memories of violation."

Don DeLillo

"Das Bedürfnis, anders zu werden als ich war, wurde plötzlich leibhaftig, wie ein Trieb."

Peter Handke

At an excessive moment you see,
as the last guest in the
projection room, when you have lost
your senses through an auricle in
a disenchanted world or overwhelmed by
faint sentiment, while you gasp for
air and, by way of abdication,
grimly bow your head into the
bath's surging stream as water churns
up like erupting thunder over the
city or in a dream that
howls like the underground or while
you study remedial gymnastics or are
upset by a glossy catalogue of
catalogues, during a car crash, in
the immense dew of Florida that
brings forth hymn after hymn from
the runner or ingloriously in the
foreboding of a bridal flight when
violence arises like a fatal, solitary
buzz over Los Alamos destroying the
heat that quivers up from an
evaporated inland sea west of Salt
Lake City, an opportunity to survive
and your heart is flooded with
joy. You shudder in your shoes.

Someone has lost count. It is
an indifferent summer. It is an
event without consequence. Your heart, veins
limbs, all jolt and tremble with
desire. Speechless, in your desolation you
fare as you so often do:
you're in love, in sexual love,
with your death and the death
of your kind. The oven you
were fatted for roars. Could the
wind lie down? Could a comparison
be made with the expanse, which
is there, where the stars are?
There's no certainty. The season slipping
by, the napalm that descends as
so many tongues, the small wonder
of six silver spoons, every little thing
— a cape, the last plum in
the icebox, a petrol station burning
to the ground, the milk that
gushes between her buttocks, the broken
jukebox — is a change, it is
an example, it shows the power
of sacrifice, displays resemblance and catastrophe
and if you do not satisfy
the desire demanded, you will die
of a ravenous passion and rave
while dying. You showed undivided attention.
You'll grow strong with enjoyment. You
no longer need to know who
these spectres in the dark are.
You've swapped the unimpressive dialectic of
light and night for the rapture
of fine-spun differences. With your external
beauty and your agitated thoughts you,
indecisively, make a perfectly natural impression.
Your sweat puts insects at ease.
So far, so good, but the
oldest fears are the worst, people

say and our breathing stifles. (*Le
désert c'est le désir*). If you
cannot see it, it must be
real. The curtain slides to one
side and your impossible journey insists
on having itself announced by force.

The pond ripples.
The pond is smooth.

*Was Faschismus seinem Wesen nach ist,
erweist sich vollständig erst dann, wenn
er die Macht besitzt und Politik
gestalten kann, also auf der Stufe
des Herrschaftssystems. Auf der Stufe der
Ideologie und der Bewegung kann sein
Wesen nur zum Teil erschlossen werden,
weil hier demagogische Elemente den realen
Charakter partiel noch verbergen.*

The pond ripples.
The pond is smooth.

"For a long time I went
to bed early, hidden in rotting
wood while the city, immersed in
nuit Américaine, was wide awake in
fear of absence and the kind
of pod that burrows tentacles as
thin as sinews through your nose,
right into your battered dream. Dare
to close your eyes and a
groping death will spread its seed
all over you. Eyes closed tightly
I became fat, white as fish-bait.
Didn't take the time to flush
out my nest. Like wasps I
left the mealy earth. Like surprised
birds. In these mental images I

swarmed out across the world. The
babbling of a crowd out of
breath making its way to the
murderously happy inertia became my nickname.
'It is I.' Yet who is
speaking? Where does the word take
place? A Doppler effect echoes through
the languages. A resounding racket had
awoken me. I revealed myself as
a public body, place of origin
without origin. I forgot my native
soil for the uncomprehending lust machines
of utter amazement, wu wei, the
mountains, non-action, the internet, the skywalks
of Minneapolis in which endless merchandise
circulates and the brutal, nuclear desert
of Nevada. I faced up to
the sun as the sun and
took from the sun its abundance."

It's darkening.
The pond ripples.

Dichtung ohne Besinnung auf Volk und
Boden ist undenkbar. Der echte Dichter
weiß im Dienst seines Volkes, dem
er verhaftet ist durch die Bande
des Blutes und der Sitte. Nationalsozialistische
Dichtung, vor allem aber ihr Gesetz,
trägt nicht der einzelne aus, sondern
der Nationalsozialismus schlechthin. Die Partei ist
nicht allein der Staat des Dritten
Reiches, sondern das Volk in seiner
Verkörperung, und sie ist das werdende
Reich.

The flower closes itself.
The pond ripples.

"I then
carried my
ashes up
into the
mountains, but
the mountains
took no
notice of
me. It
was I,
the one
in which
was expressed:
'If you
do not
produce what
is in
you, then
what you
do not
produce will
annihilate you.'
Yet I
was what
I produced
and what
I was
I did
not know.
No more
than how
in I
was in
me. And
how little
I was
I how
I the
manifold names

from history
that I
was not
than on
that single
lasting day,
beaten in
enjoyment outside
your countable
rational calendar,
in Ash
Springs, a
wide, baseless
petrol station,
a vortex
later repeating
itself. It
was a
place full
of power
and danger.
Tree roots
I ate,
baked beans,
salted meat
and chilli
burritos under
this expanse
like hammered
copper plate,
from which,
when I
walked around,
the waters
of chaos
and darkness
descended. I
could see
the Nevada

Test Site
as the
west, even
with eyes
sewn shut
behind the
screen door.
I had
(in what
disposition?) gone
into the
deep south.
That deep,
desperate south
welled up
in me
like soil
shadowed by
blood. I
could no
longer separate
soul and
senses. *'Hey
Bill, I
heard you
shot your
woman down'*.
Then my
body was
discarded, like
a bush
burning and
unconsumed, a
hotbed, hot
in hot
grass. And
now? My
assorted tormentors,
what now?"

The pond is smooth.
The pond ripples.

Der Faschismus an der Macht ist
die äußerste Systemsicherung in äußersten Krisenlagen
des monopolbestimmten Kapitalismus. In den entwickelten
kapitalistischen Ländern besteht die Hauptfunktion faschistischer
Ideologien, Gruppen und Aktivitäten darin, Unterstützung
für eine rechtsorientierte (auf stärker autoritär
bestimmte Herrschaftsmethoden und auf Militarisierung der
Gesellschaft gerichtete) Politik zu liefern.

The pond ripples.
The foliage cheers.

Start again with the sun, sailing towards the void, a pure event, a
catastrophe without gift of mercy or 'powerful voice'. No religion's
involved in this. No anthropomorphisms. 'In four billion years
your phenomenology and utopian politics will have died out,
with no one remaining to sound the death knell or hear it.' Nature
ignores our existence, this much is clear. That leaves the question
whether you are, here and now, having a sore throat, caressing
her shaven mound, smelling petrol fumes, feeding the cats or are,
as Harrison Ford in *Blade Runner*, in the dark about your 'life'.
Perhaps you are, like Deckard 'on the run' through the chemical
rain of L.A., an actor's character that's after you, a replicant with
emotions, dreams, a case history. A story programmed many times
(by whom?), set in a darkened city. Impatient. Delusional. You
don't see things unfolded or in their entirety, but in likenesses.
Against a background of other likenesses. Luckily there is the self-
destructing clock inside of you. The question is therefore: how
long, who to spend time with and what for? In that light everything
is without consequence.

The pond. The pond.
Ripples. Is smooth.

Sein soziales Wesen realisiert der Faschismus
durch die terroristische Zerschlagung der Organisationen

der abhängig Arbeitenden, durch die Auflösung
oder Entmachtung aller anderen Organisationen, in
denen antimonopolistische Interessen sich artikulieren könnten,
durch die Abschaffung der Institutionen des
Parlamentarismus und der rechtsstaatlichen Bindungen des
Staatsapparates, durch die Zentralisierung der politischen
Macht und durch die Errichtung eines
Systems umfassender Kontrolle aller Lebensbereichen.

The pond reflects
reflects the pond.

"The pain of thinking is, I
think, thinking itself to the extent
that it decides to be indecisive.
Who saw the wind, loudly breathing
signifier of the event? The chaos
that lives in us. The charge
that chases you before the tepid
lightning of pipe dreams and forces
us to continually evaluate positions and
decisions? Is he the disregarded one
who, like whizzing bamboo, gives us
a slap on the soles of
our feet when nodding off flares
up in us like a blush?
The not now not ever? And *what*
blows through the fading that announces
itself in a mood (that *tangible*
emotion), flows out 'heavy' as passion
as well as 'confusion'? The eventful
that even parodies its own model,
interrupts you like anaesthesia? Only when
the model changes can we learn
from history. You there, with your
statements, your irony: know what effaces
you, makes your body an anonymous
place of excess, discipline. Political, beside
itself, sweating under its weight without

ideals. In days of almost 'perfect
composure' it presents itself as horny
and disturbing like a professionally administered
enema in the rubber room. Such
was my belief in earthly beauty,
human autonomy as celebrated in antique
books. If I am wild, it's
because life, that's earthly, is wild."

Your oldest fears are the worst.
A strong black rain is descending.

*"Um die Unterjochung der Kolonialvölker zu
legitimieren und die Bevölkerung für den
Krieg zu mobilisieren, war die aus
dem kapitalistischen Konkurrenzkampf relativ spontan entstehende
Ideologie des Sozialdarwinismus zu einem extremen
Nationalismus und Rassismus gesteigert und durch
effektivierte ideologische Apparate verbreitet worden."*

The flower closes itself. The pond.
The state's monopoly on violence.

"I left 'my native soil'
for a yielding world,
without truth or reality,
but living, solid on
details. Flourishing in faces
like swarms of midges,
paragrams, a serene progress
shows itself as swaying
that disappears into old
city light, blind maps,
partial connections, the blissful
cotton that lifts a
bed wide into the
night, Chaplin's hilarious eating
machine. Ecstasy without consequence.
The rest that remains

when all has been
said, perhaps fulfils itself
in the banal thud
of steel on steel
or like a slowly
unfurling fireball that climbs
the Nevada sky, singing.
In a different state
of history that was
a pillar in the
east, an encampment exploring
frontiers, a bricked up
church niche, a dream
palace in the opium
slumber of a nineteenth-century
body. Is this it,
trembling lust organ? High-pitched
wedding song? Behind the
throbbing blue of the
Lincoln sand wafted up.
Radio reception was perfect
and from Callas' singing
elsewhere flowed 'Ne andro
lontana' as a precious,
sad body. In draughty
airports passengers embarked. For
a destination. People sat
awake at night, applauding
the news. Sang a
hymn to the nation:
an invasion being prepared.
These heroes fight for
freedom. High-rises started to
dominate the cityscape. But
for years I never
grew tired of enjoyment,
hindered by no heart's
desire, stunned by the
Internet's byways through which

I ran my Oraciones
(or vice versa), becoming
other people's complex allusions,
meanwhile consumed by an
expensive, personal sun, a
virus that annuls its
host: white light, white
heat. Once there was
stuff, shot, rush, the
echo of a shot.
A high tone whined
on through the world,
awakening in the cry
of everyone startled by
a nightmare. A whistling
cocktail glass fell, fell,
fell. What once drove
you breathlessly into a
body? Led us choking
like fish from the
dream. Everything changes, but
in death's direction. You're
a being that should be
blinded and stunned. '*If*
we realize that everything
is illusion, then any
illusion is perfect.' The
Continental took me where
the Continental wanted. Stately
body, wrathful orchestra, lethal
construction in which I
lost myself unknowingly and,
breathing broadly, could ascertain
the shape-shifting world that
displaced in its unnameability
and struck down and
struck down I was
allowed to shift. This
was Nevada, a wilderness

blooming with drought, plutonium,
lust. In the machine
I sat chalk-white as
Buster Keaton dragged by
a train. A Texaco
signpost creaked to and
fro in the silence.
The wind blew incessantly
about the pump. Grass
gnawed its way through
the cracks in the
concrete. Welcome. Garage, body
shop, sacrificial site to
the sun. The wind
was petrol, drenched your
clothes, your hair, breath
and soul. This was
the placeless place that
had called me. I
took my placeless residence
there and the place
went into me. A
shudder ran through the
immediate vicinity. It resembled
'the soft sough of
a breeze' or 'the
frail sound of silence'.
It was perhaps a
descending owl or the
thick rush of blood
in the inner ear
of someone who, quadriplegically,
sees all this take
root in him as
his salvation, his oldest
fear or the interminably
slow telescoping of steel,
tank, skin, burning rubber
in a crash that

permanently repeats itself in
this protracted screaming, resembling
the delayed sound reproduction
of Canticles or the
stronger being of an
angel who impatiently fingered
your soul's sphincter. The
desert demanded my constant
rapture and the sun
did its job: the
Lincoln became malleable steel
in the heat; my
nasal bone hardened into
titanium. The wind bashed
gills into my ribs.
I snarled at the
sun, which wrote its
punishment into my muscles.
A body's remains having
struck down on the
engine block. Swarming with
flies, it was without
organs and smooth. Latched
onto it from miles
around jackals, maggots, organ
creatures and signs. Rods
penetrated holes. Pistons and
tubes connected to the
bloodstream. Greased up creases.
(A fist-size gear-stick shone
in its mouth.) Chrome,
flywheel, transmission. It spoke
with one armpit, breathed
difficultly through wafting hair.
Angry in its angry
appearance it stared unreasoningly
at the ruins of
history from an anus
related to the sun,

retched blood, sperm, petrol.
Was rapture now conceivable
as an idea of
place? It was all
undone with flow charts,
flight paths, turmoil, sweat,
logograms, geodesics and tar.
A body became body
without organization, while thousands
of ants sprayed their
pheromones groggily onto blazing
skin, a chemical vocabulary
that spurts in dreams,
territorial marks as unspeakable
as lust. The beauty
of thresholds here in
the heat. No postponement
of death or nullity.
Traces, formulas, fall-out, a
punch: it was taking
place, raving. It was
midnight and the rain
beat against the window-panes.
It wasn't midnight and
the rain didn't beat
against the window-panes. I
saw all enjoyment in
the raving of love.
It was enjoyment beyond
comprehension. Moderation exists, for
I am excess: I
was ablaze last night,
people could almost see
I had died. I
seemed radioactive last night
and am nowhere to
be found. Start again
with the sun, an
imperceptible catastrophe. The end

will carry the burden.
The lust for lust
lies somewhere in between."

The pond is smooth:
the order is not to move.

Der Nationalsozialismus als Wille zur Hochwertigkeit
entspricht geradezu der Tragödie, die höchste
Lebensbejahung ist. Die Gemeinschaftstragik unterscheidet sich
gerade dadurch von der Individualtragik, daß
sie den Helden in die Basis
des Handelns des ganzen Volkes stellt,
das heißt, den Helden mit dem
sittlich notwendigen Ideal identifiziert.

It's darkening?
Rule out any ambivalence!

"In those days
I sat on
the veranda, circumsphinxed
by Dudu and
Suleika, two feline
raiders, red-eyed, thin,
sexless in their
comings and goings,
wedded closely to
the fluttering world,
the planet taking
its first breaths
that became flesh.
Guarding the intensity
of the unimportant.
Pliable. Gladly circling
petrol tanks. In
the morning sun
my 360 joints
spoke to the

plaintive awakening of
their cartilage in
the language of
seed-boxes popping open
or a pinery
bursting into flame.
I lay there
getting all benevolent
when, like water
rushing down, Ariel
stood behind me,
panting in a
midnight jacket. In
backlight I saw
his hair streaming
silver-white, one of
Blake's illustrations. The
jaw the jaw
of an effigy.
The moon in
his iron teeth.
I thought, some
perverse order's emerging
when, trumpeting (a
megaphone?), he spoke
to me: "You'll
write history if
you do business."
I thought, what
a great opening
and said, looking
at the boney
flapper behind his
zipper: "Is that
a gun in
your pocket or
are you just
happy to see
me?" A whirlwind

rose, sucked the
blackness from the
world. It whirled
around in his
eyes, smoked from
his throat, fluttered
down. His briefcase
appeared to produce
a lead pipe.
Quick as lightning.
He struck like
an animal, for
seconds, that was
a clause in
his contract. My
night eyes, fits
of pain, delusion
breeders, didn't escape:
chucked Dudu into
orbit, Suleika rocked,
quite flattened, towards
the pavement. The
cities were lifeless.
Water dripped from
bridges while Ariel
shiningly continued, dancing
orderly within the
law that made
him part of
an erasing force,
spoken in a
language that pushes
us down and
wreaks havoc deep
within us, finger
pointed imperatively at
me: *"Say after*
me: — I pledge
allegiance to the

flag of the
United States of
America, to the
Republic for which
it stands, one
nation under God,
indivisible, with liberty
and justice for
all." I saw
the landscape as
Sinai, leaning back,
humming, until slime,
fat, piss, vermin,
snot, all broke
out of me.
It left me
spontaneously, my prayer
to God. Around
me swarmed (his?)
midnight creatures and
Ariel smashed through
all the doors,
dragged me, bucking,
bawling, roaring, away
through the heavens,
showed me all
the world's kingdoms,
bathing in glory.
Said: "All these
things will I
give thee, with
thine grease-reflecting hair,
bugger, self-igniter, when
thee kneelest before
me in worship,
abandon all pleasures,
say after me:
'— *It's patriotic to*
have the AIDS

test and be
negative.'" Blood streamed
out of my
ears and eyes.
I vomited all
over his shoes.
I shat in
his pockets, roared
with laughter. Swayed
like Erroll Flynn
across the scene.
Beamed. Became woman.
So he immediately
(being quick-witted) knelt
down before the
sink in an
elegant tuxedo as
if at an
altar vast in
the evening light
or flickering neon.
A Vegas organ
started the dance.
And he spoke:
"Say after me:
I take you,
to have and
to hold, from
this day forward,
for better for
worse, for richer
for poorer, in
sickness and in
health, to love
and to cherish,
till death do
us part, so
help me God."
He drank from

the chalice, breathed
heavily as if
already consummating our
marriage. But when
it passed, singing,
through my hands
I smelt petrol.
How could it
be otherwise? Took
a swig. Trembling
(with distaste, anticipation,
distraction, unrest?) I
lit the first
Lucky Strike of
the day." Wwwwwhhhooosshh
sang the diva.

And so the landscape
became ever stranger
The pond
The flowers
The boyum tree
Doodadoodoodadoo
Yackety yack
Doodadoodoodadoo
Yackety yack
The clouds wide
and white, the
clouds wide
and white, the clouds
wide and white, the clouds wide and
white
If this is the real world
you can keep it
How can you only
Who is the dearly departed?
You sleep and you think
that you are safe
but in the dark

I'm standing beside you and you don't know what
The violence lies hidden
The catastrophe
is what we forget to think
You're walking in the wrong direction
She spread her arms and
Be bop a lula, she's my baby
If I could only
Try to get used to my company,
I even have friendly dreams
that have always
started elsewhere, earlier, differently
You close your eyes and when you open them
you think that everything must have changed
I am totally ready for it
I can at least show my teeth
She thinks that she'd better
She turned round
It's as if,
Do not pretend
Join us now
It is high time
Soon in a cinema near you
You are so far away
Such is life on earth

Appendix to 'Wwwhhhooossshhh'

Translations of the German texts:

Page 95, epigraph:
"The need to be other than I really was suddenly became physical, like desire."

Page 97:
The real character of Fascism is
only made completely manifest when
it attains power and can construct
policy, in other words when it attains the level
of a ruling system. At the level of
ideology and movement its character
can only be partly revealed,
because here demagogic elements still partly
obscure its real character.

Page 98:
Writing that reflects neither the people nor
the soil is unthinkable. The real poet
knows [that he is] in the service of his people, to whom
he is shackled by the bonds of
blood and custom. National Socialist
writing, above all however, its laws,
is not delivered by the individual, but
by National Socialism itself, pure and simple. The Party is
not just the State of the Third
Reich; it is the embodiment of
the people, and it is the nascent
Reich.

Page 102:
Fascism in power is
the most extreme safety valve in monopoly capitalism's
most extreme moment of crisis. In developed
capitalist countries the chief function of fascist

ideologies, groups, activities lies in the delivery of support
for rightist policies (those directed towards
a strongly authoritarian ruling style
and the militarisation of society).

Page 102-103:
Fascism realises its social character
through the terrorist suppression of the independent
workforce's organisations, through the break-up
or removal from power of all other organisations in
which anti-monopolistic interests could express themselves,
through the abolition of Parliamentary
institutions and of the State's subordination
to the rule of law, through the centralisation of political
power and through the construction of a
system of comprehensive control over all areas of life.

Page 104:
"In order to legitimise the subjugation of
colonial peoples and to mobilise the
populace for war, the ideology of social darwinism —
more or less spontaneously derived from capitalism's
competitive struggle — had developed into an extreme form
of nationalism and racism and was disseminated
through effective ideological means."

Page 110:
National Socialism as the will to high value
is directly in accordance with tragedy, which is the highest
affirmation of life. Communal tragedy differs
from individual tragedy exactly because of this: because
it places the hero at the grass-roots
of the entire people's activity,
that is to say, it identifies the hero
with the required moral ideal.

Printed in the United Kingdom
by Lightning Source UK Ltd.
103862UKS00001B/190-282